You Can Make a Dinosaur and........ Eat It Too!

Margaret E. Westin and Norman W. Westin

I CORN / F3K Productions, Ltd., Mt. Kisco, N.Y.

CONTENTS

Welcome.. 1
Why We Developed Our "no-cook" snack book.......... 1
Kitchen Safety... 2
Teamwork.. 2
Food Guide Pyramid.................................. 3
Recipe Rectangle..................................... 3
Food Substitutions................................... 3
Glue Foods.. 4
Children's Supplies.................................. 4
Snack-tivities...What are they?.................... 5
Recipes and Their Related Snack-tivities........... 6-29
Cutting and Preparation Ideas...................... 30-35
More Snack Ideas..................................... 36
Snack-tivity Pages and Recipes an Index............ 37
Thank you.. 38

Note: When you see the initials **"CACFP"** on a page, this means that the recipe meets the **CHILD + ADULT CARE FOOD PROGRAM** guidelines as listed for snacks for 3-5 year olds under the rules of this Federal (U.S. Dept. of Agriculture) Program. Because of the size of some pieces used, however, we recommend that our recipes be prepared with children 4 years of age or older.

Snack-tivity Pages and Recipes

Put-Together Creations

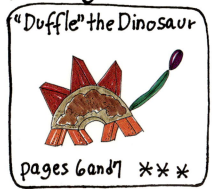

"Duffle" the Dinosaur

pages 6 and 7 ✳ ✳ ✳

"Baby Grape's" Carriage

pages 8 and 9 ✳ ✳ ✳

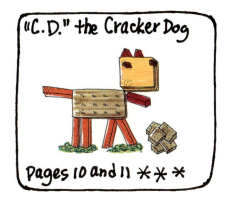

"C.D." the Cracker Dog

Pages 10 and 11 ✳ ✳ ✳

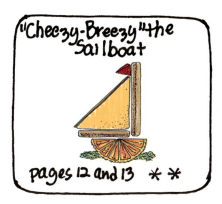

"Cheezy-Breezy" the Sailboat

Pages 12 and 13 ✳ ✳

"Creamy" the Sheep

pages 14 and 15 ✳

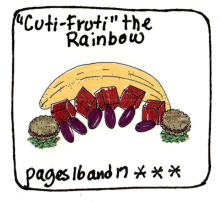

"Cuti-Fruti" the Rainbow

pages 16 and 17 ✳ ✳ ✳

"Icy" the Snowman

pages 18 and 19 ✳

"Lettuce tail" the Pony

pages 20 and 21 ✳ ✳

"Little Bite" the Teddy Bear

pages 22 and 23 ✳

"Pepper horn the Bull

Pages 24 and 25 ✳ ✳ ✳

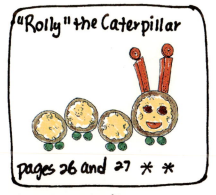

"Rolly" the Caterpillar

pages 26 and 27 ✳ ✳

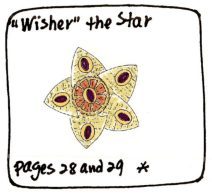

"Wisher" the Star

Pages 28 and 29 ✳

✳ Meets CACFP snack requirements for bread and fruit
✳ ✳ Meets CACFP snack requirements for bread and meat alternative
✳ ✳ ✳ Meets CACFP snack requirements for bread, fruit/vegetable, and meat alternative

Our Thanks To:

The many children who helped to make this book possible through their creative input, taste testing and great ideas. Some of those children include: Carissa and Kyle Eichhorn, Kristi and Courtney Farrell, Catherine Lavin, Liam McLaughlin, Ian and Matthew Luke, Megan O'Donoghue, and Diana and Gregory Westin.
A special thank you to our junior chefs: Keeley Boehmer and Andrew Santora.

Some of the adults who provided great input include: Jean Chandler, Audrey, Patricia, John and Richard Eichhorn, Mary Farrell, Valorie Luke, Sue Peckman, Ana Standard, Betty Walde, Joyce and Dr. Ray Wall.

To the people who helped us with the graphics: Beverly Aherns and Eileen Kirtz

For his inspirational guidance: The Reverend Jack Traugett

Wow! We are really grateful to you all. · Margaret and Norman Westin

WELCOME to a new kind of snack food book that
was developed for kids of all ages to enjoy. It can be used as a picture book by the very youngest child and as a snack food recipe book by children as young as 4 YEARS OLD.

WHEN it is used as a snack food recipe book, it is important that an
complete certain tasks for the child, such as the handling of knives in the cutting and peeling of fruits and vegetables.

ADULT HELPER

WHY WE DEVELOPED OUR "NO-COOK" Book

These recipes are organized so that children can have as much independence as possible in creating FUN food snacks. They can be made from foods commonly found in most kitchens and include but are not limited to:

carrots   apples   bananas   bread   peas

WITH this book even the youngest child can enjoy learning how to make snacks that
contain healthy everyday foods.

KITCHEN SAFETY

SAFETY REMINDERS

1. Wash hands before beginning
2. Wash all fruits and vegetables you are planning to use
3. Work on a clean surface
4. Refrigerate foods that could spoil
   (such as cottage cheese, ricotta cheese, yogurt)
5. Clean up food preparation area when you are finished

PLEASE REMEMBER: ADULT HELPERS need to do certain tasks for children such as cutting with sharp knives (see pages 30-35 for cutting ideas).

TEAM WORK

The recipes in this book are intended to be used by an ADULT HELPER working with a child or GROUP of CHILDREN.

Some Team Tasks:

Choosing the recipe... making the shopping list... buying the ingredients... washing the fruits and vegetables... peeling the fruits and vegetables... tearing or cutting the lettuce... spreading the "glue foods"... assembling the food project... eating the snack together... cleaning up.

FOOD GUIDE PYRAMID

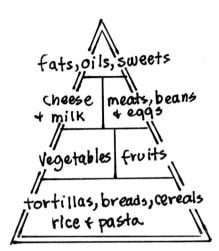

fats, oils, sweets

cheese + milk | meats, beans + eggs

Vegetables | fruits

tortillas, breads, cereals rice + pasta

Developed by the U.S. Department of Agriculture, the FOOD GUIDE PYRAMID is intended to help adults and children make good food choices. Adults and children should choose most of their foods from the three lower sections of the pyramid and limit their intake of foods found in the small tip (on the top) of the pyramid.

RECIPE RECTANGLE

Most children have been able to complete the food design by just looking at the illustration and picking out the number of pieces needed of a particular food simply by counting and identifying the kind and number of pieces that they find in the BLUE RECIPE RECTANGLE

FOOD SUBSTITUTIONS

If the child is allergic to a particular food shown in the recipe, it is IMPORTANT to substitute a food that is acceptable. Food substitutions can be a fun way to develop a new food idea or taste.

GLUE FOODS

WE call the foods that are suitable for holding sandwiches and food design parts together "GLUE FOODS".

WE recommend that you use these:

cottage cheese
ricotta cheese
yogurt
peanut butter or
nut butters

and, on occasion, butter, cream cheese and whipped cream.

CHILDREN'S SUPPLIES

The cooking supplies needed by children are minimal. Most tasks can be completed by using a plastic spoon or plastic knife or even a wooden popsicle stick to assemble the snacks on a 9" paper plate.

SNACK-TIVITIES

WHAT ARE THEY?

EACH illustrated recipe has its own SNACK-TIVITY PAGE. On the page opposite the illustration, you will find these helpful ideas.

FOOD PATTERNS ○▯▢△ ⠿ ◠ ⊡

These are full-sized outlines of the food pieces needed for each recipe. Since foods often vary in size, color and shape from the illustrations, you may find these patterns a helpful aid in measuring food pieces.

FOOD FOR THOUGHT ????

You can use these questions to learn more about different foods, shapes, and colors.

STEP-BY-STEP 1-2-3-4-5-6

These outline pictures can serve as a guide in placing the food pieces on the plate in the numbered order listed.

"Duffle"© the Dinosaur
Snack-tivities

Food Patterns

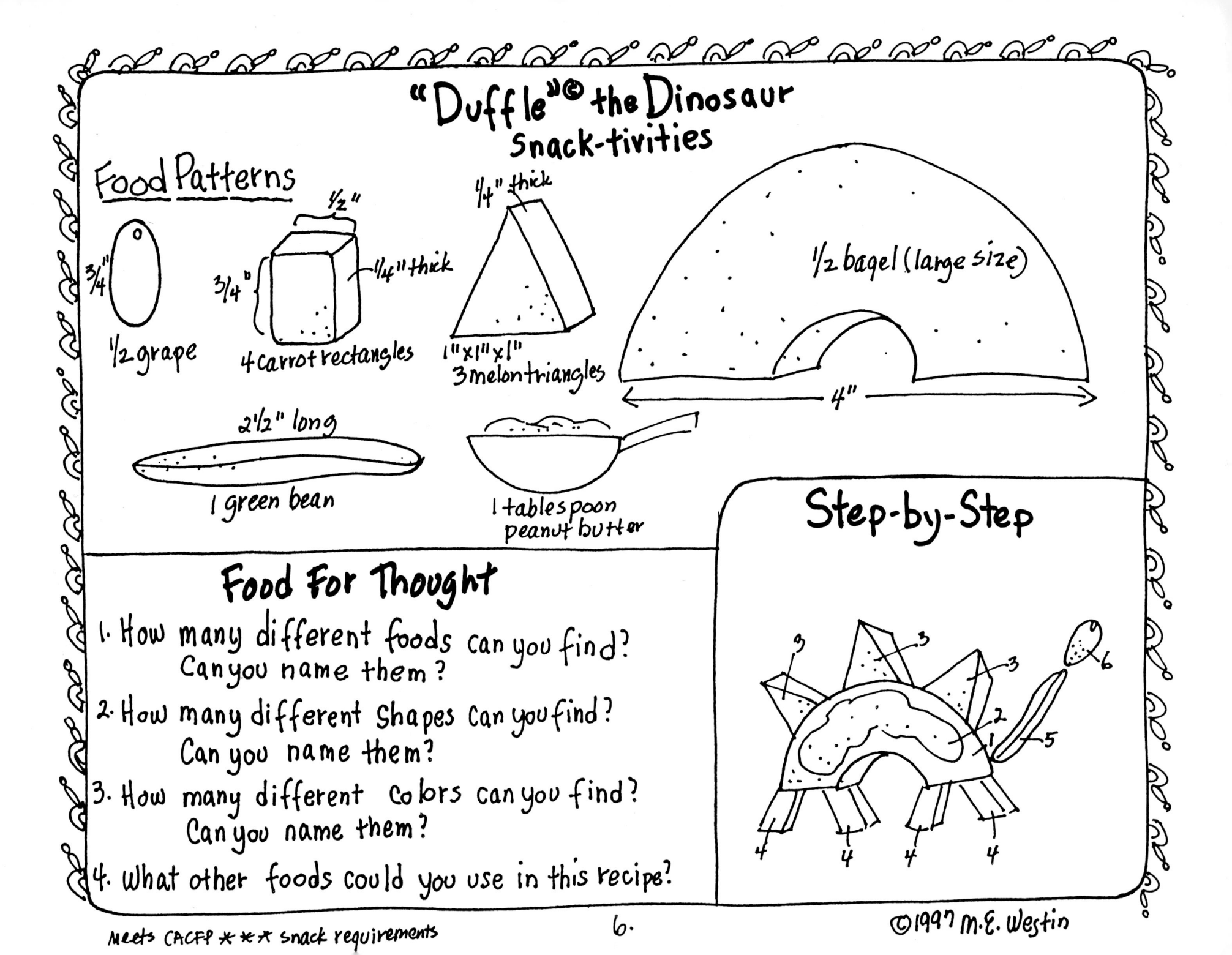

3/4" — 1/2 grape

1/2"
3/4" — 1/4" thick
4 carrot rectangles

1/4" thick
1"x1"x1"
3 melon triangles

1/2 bagel (large size)
4"

2 1/2" long
1 green bean

1 tablespoon peanut butter

Step-by-Step

Food For Thought

1. How many different foods can you find? Can you name them?

2. How many different shapes can you find? Can you name them?

3. How many different colors can you find? Can you name them?

4. What other foods could you use in this recipe?

©1997 M.E. Westin

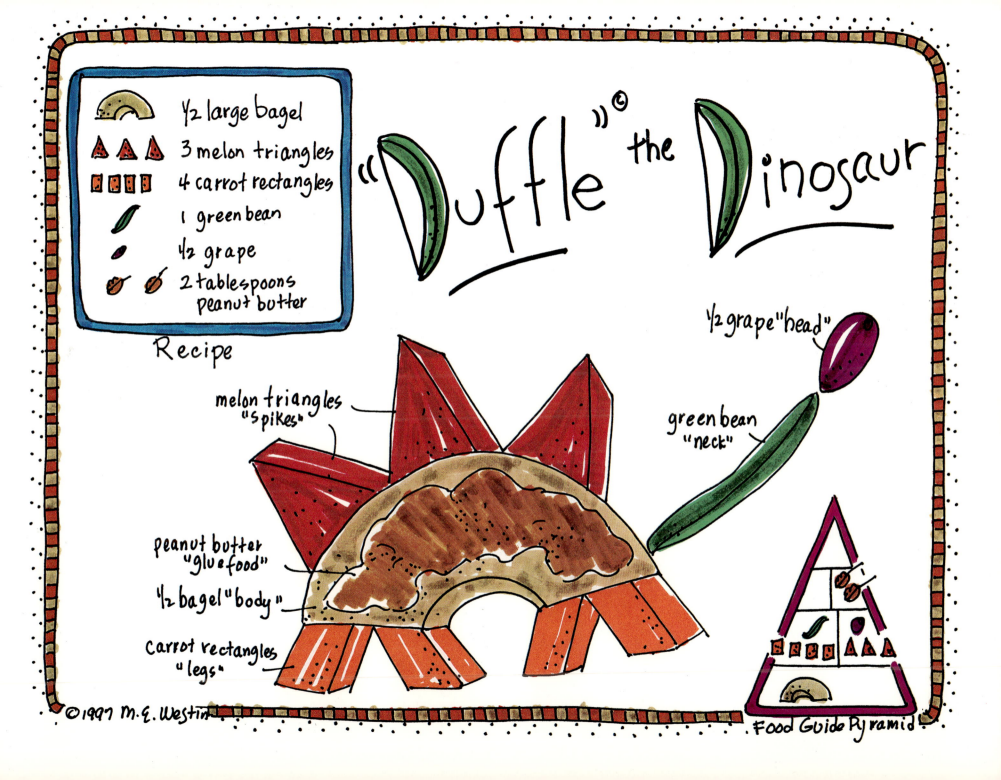

"Duffle" the Dinosaur

Recipe

- ½ large bagel
- 3 melon triangles
- 4 carrot rectangles
- 1 green bean
- ½ grape
- 2 tablespoons peanut butter

½ grape "head"

green bean "neck"

melon triangles "spikes"

peanut butter "glue food"

½ bagel "body"

carrot rectangles "legs"

Food Guide Pyramid

©1997 M.E. Westin

"Baby grape's"© carriage
Snack-tivities

peanut butter

1 tablespoon

Food Patterns

$\frac{7}{8}$" round

$\frac{3}{4}$"

½ large grape

$\frac{1}{4}$" thick

2 banana circles

1 apple Wedge

$1\frac{1}{2}$"

1" thick

3" long

1 green bean

$\frac{1}{4}$" thick

3"

½ orange slice

1 thick bread stick $4\frac{1}{2}$" long   ½" thick

Food For Thought

1. How many different foods can you find?
   Can you name them?

2. How many different shapes can you find?
   Can you name them?

3. How many different colors can you find?
   Can you name them?

4. What other foods could you use in this recipe?

Step-by-Step

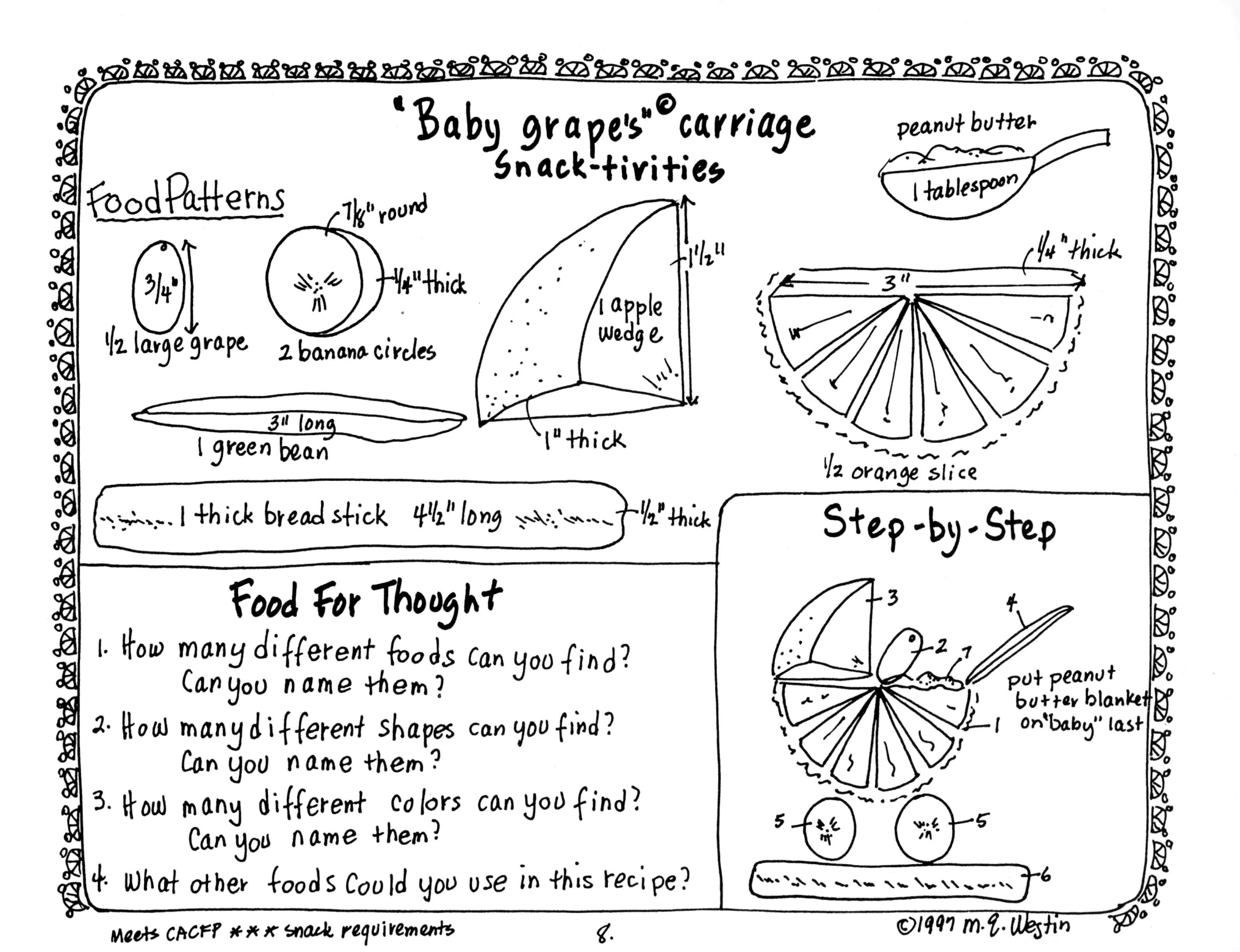

put peanut butter blanket on "baby" last

"Baby grape's"©

Carriage

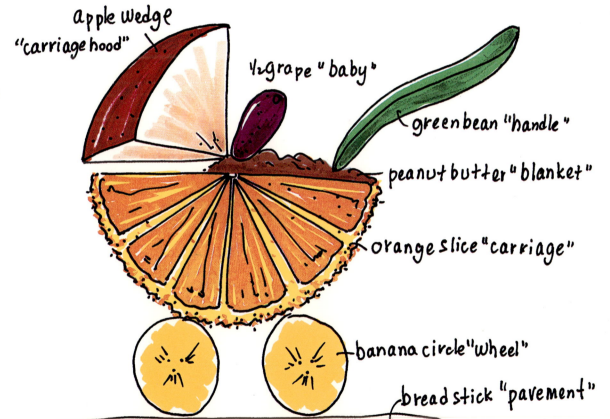

apple wedge
"carriage hood"

½ grape "baby"

green bean "handle"

peanut butter "blanket"

orange slice "carriage"

banana circle "wheel"

bread stick "pavement"

1 apple wedge

½ orange slice

½ grape

1 green bean

2 banana circles

1 fat bread stick

1 tablespoon peanut butter

Recipe

Food Guide Pyramid

©1997 M.C. Westin

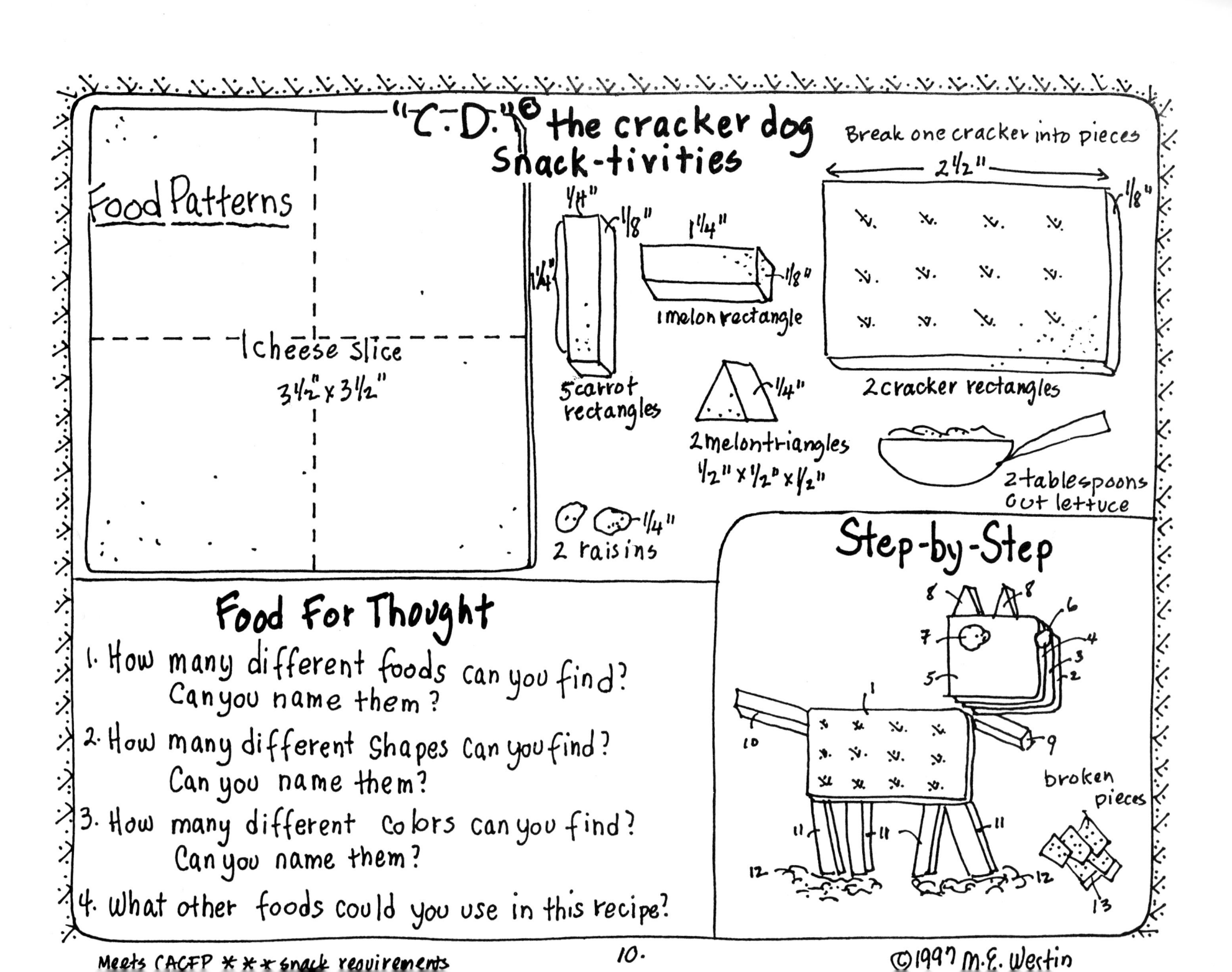

"C.D." the cracker dog
Snack-tivities

Food Patterns

1 cheese slice
3½" x 3½"

5 carrot rectangles
¼" ⅛" ¼"

1 melon rectangle
1¼" ⅛"

2 melon triangles
½" x ½" x ½"

Break one cracker into pieces
2½" ⅛"

2 cracker rectangles

2 tablespoons cut lettuce

2 raisins ¼"

Food For Thought

1. How many different foods can you find? Can you name them?

2. How many different shapes can you find? Can you name them?

3. How many different colors can you find? Can you name them?

4. What other foods could you use in this recipe?

Step-by-Step

broken pieces

Meets CACFP * * * snack requirements   ©1997 M.E. Westin

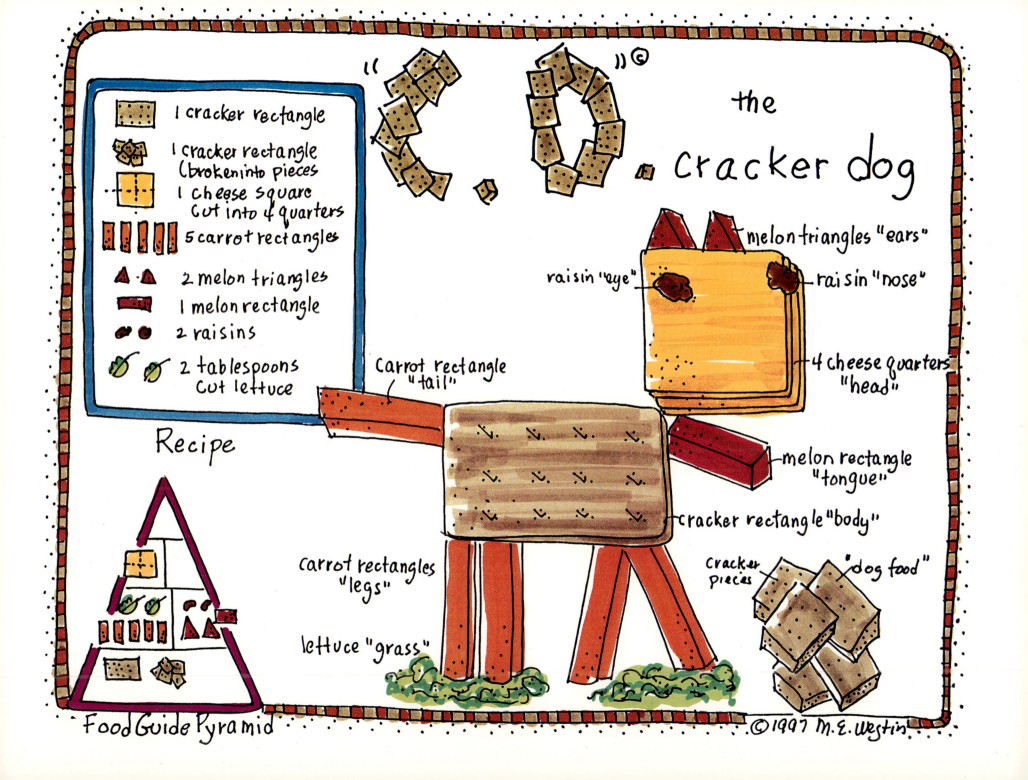

"C.D."© the cracker dog

Legend / ingredients:

- 1 cracker rectangle
- 1 cracker rectangle (broken into pieces)
- 1 cheese square cut into 4 quarters
- 5 carrot rectangles
- 2 melon triangles
- 1 melon rectangle
- 2 raisins
- 2 tablespoons cut lettuce

Recipe

Food Guide Pyramid

Labels on the dog:
- melon triangles "ears"
- raisin "eye"
- raisin "nose"
- 4 cheese quarters "head"
- Carrot rectangle "tail"
- melon rectangle "tongue"
- cracker rectangle "body"
- carrot rectangles "legs"
- cracker pieces "dog food"
- lettuce "grass"

©1997 M. E. Westin

"Cheezy-Breezy" the Sailboat
Snack-tivities

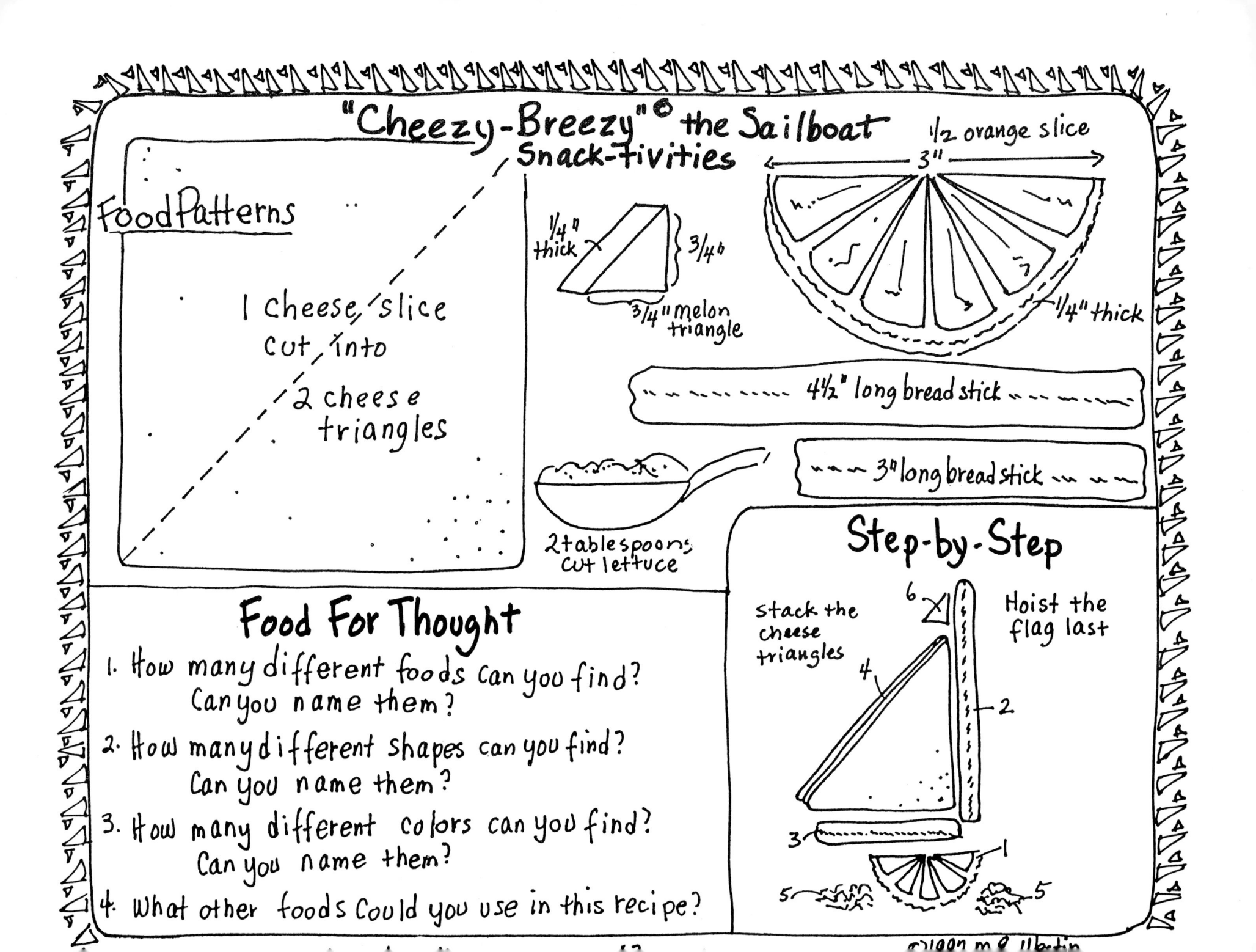

Food Patterns

1 cheese slice cut into

2 cheese triangles

1/4" thick

3/4"

3/4" melon triangle

1/2 orange slice

3"

1/4" thick

4 1/2" long bread stick

3" long bread stick

2 tablespoons cut lettuce

Step-by-Step

stack the cheese triangles

Hoist the flag last

6

4

2

3

1

5

5

Food For Thought

1. How many different foods can you find? Can you name them?

2. How many different shapes can you find? Can you name them?

3. How many different colors can you find? Can you name them?

4. What other foods could you use in this recipe?

©1997 M & J Martin

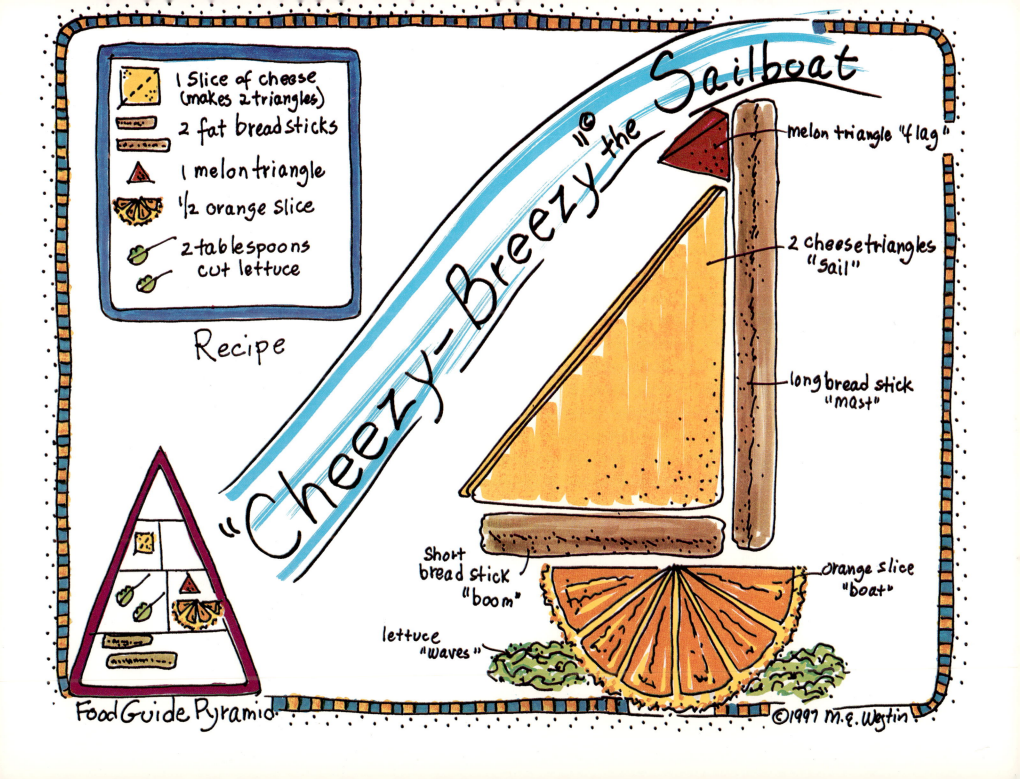

"Cheezy-Breezy" the Sailboat

Recipe

1 Slice of cheese (makes 2 triangles)

2 fat bread sticks

1 melon triangle

½ orange slice

2 tablespoons cut lettuce

melon triangle "flag"

2 cheese triangles "Sail"

long bread stick "mast"

Short bread stick "boom"

orange slice "boat"

lettuce "waves"

Food Guide Pyramid

©1997 M.E. Wytin

"Creamy"© the Sheep
Snack-tivities

FoodPatterns

5 raisins

4 pretzel sticks
1"

4 apple wedges
1¼"
¾"
1¼"

2¼"
2 oval crackers

3 banana circles

2 tablespoons whipped cream

Step-by-Step

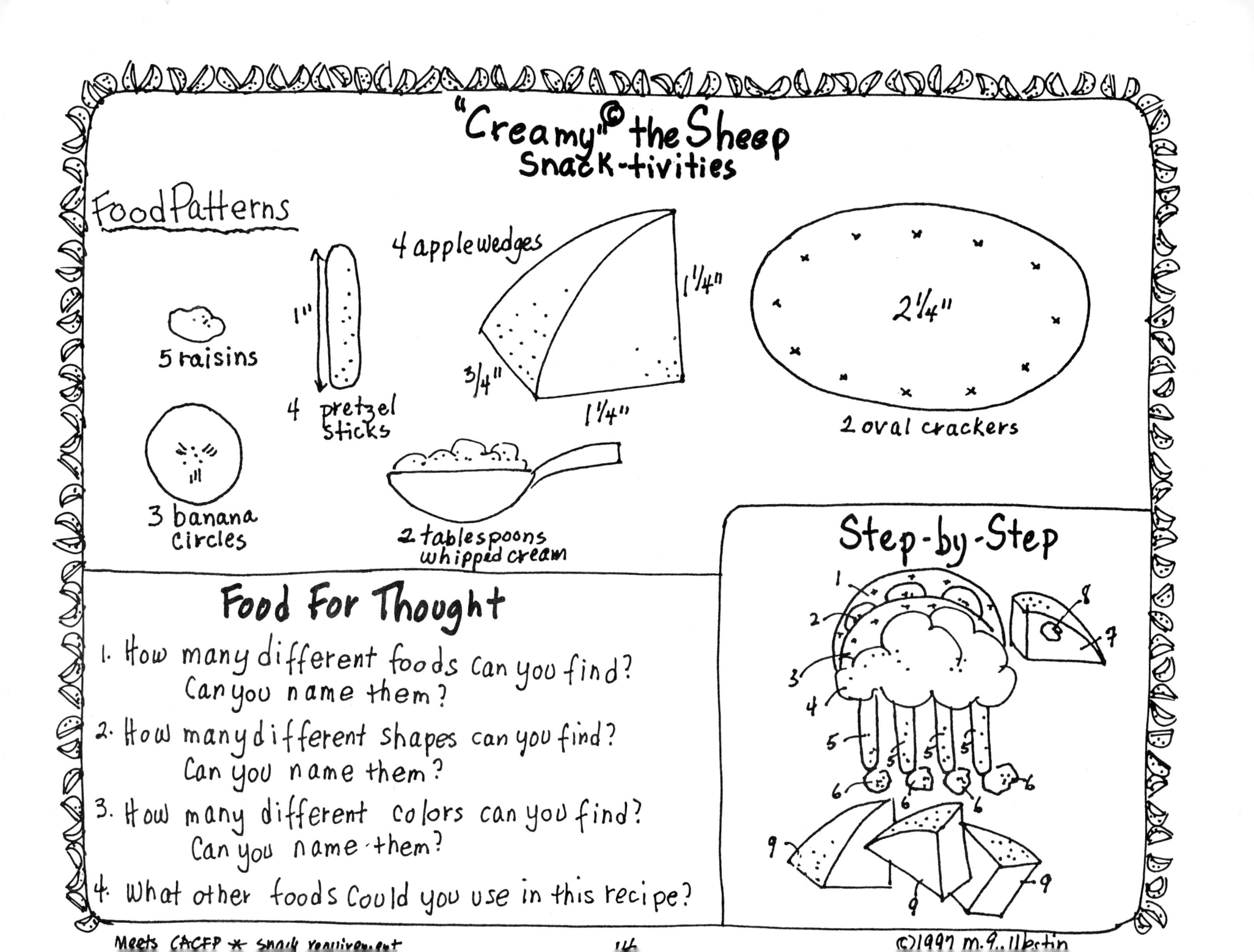

Food For Thought

1. How many different foods can you find? Can you name them?

2. How many different shapes can you find? Can you name them?

3. How many different colors can you find? Can you name them?

4. What other foods could you use in this recipe?

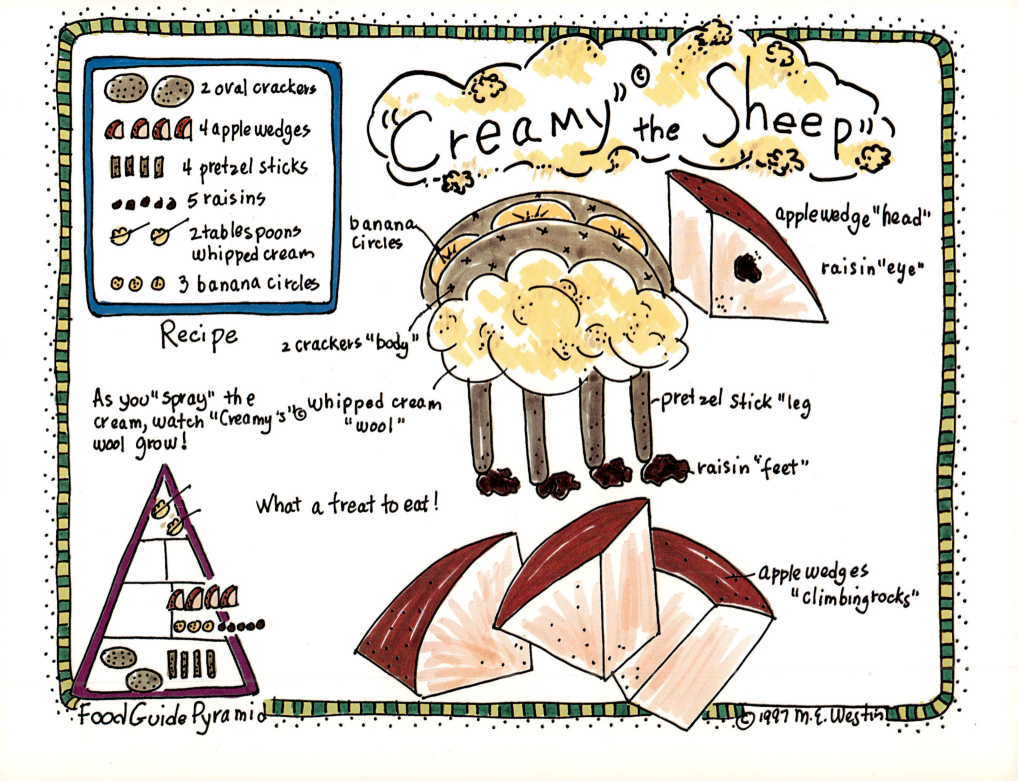

"Creamy" the "Sheep"

2 oval crackers

4 apple wedges

4 pretzel sticks

5 raisins

2 tablespoons whipped cream

3 banana circles

Recipe

As you "spray" the cream, watch "Creamy's"© wool grow!

What a treat to eat!

banana circles

2 crackers "body"

whipped cream "wool"

apple wedge "head"

raisin "eye"

pretzel stick "leg

raisin "feet"

apple wedges "climbing rocks"

Food Guide Pyramid

© 1997 M.E. Westin

"Cuti-Fruti"© the Rainbow
Snack-tivities

Food Patterns

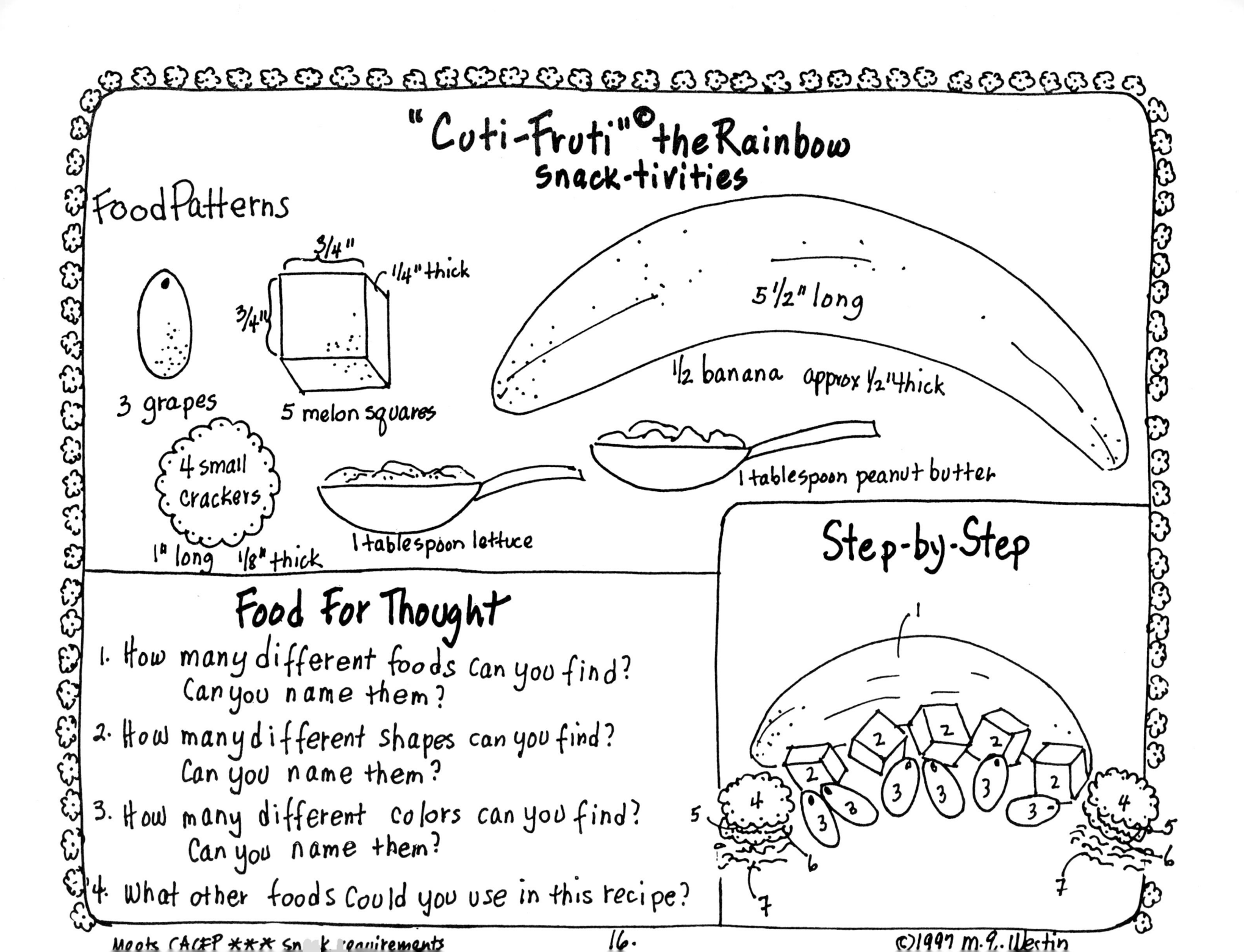

3 grapes

3/4"
3/4"
1/4" thick

5 melon squares

4 small crackers

1" long   1/8" thick

1 tablespoon lettuce

5 1/2" long

1/2 banana   approx 1/2" thick

1 tablespoon peanut butter

Step-by-Step

Food For Thought

1. How many different foods can you find? Can you name them?

2. How many different shapes can you find? Can you name them?

3. How many different colors can you find? Can you name them?

4. What other foods could you use in this recipe?

Meets CACFP *** Snack requirements

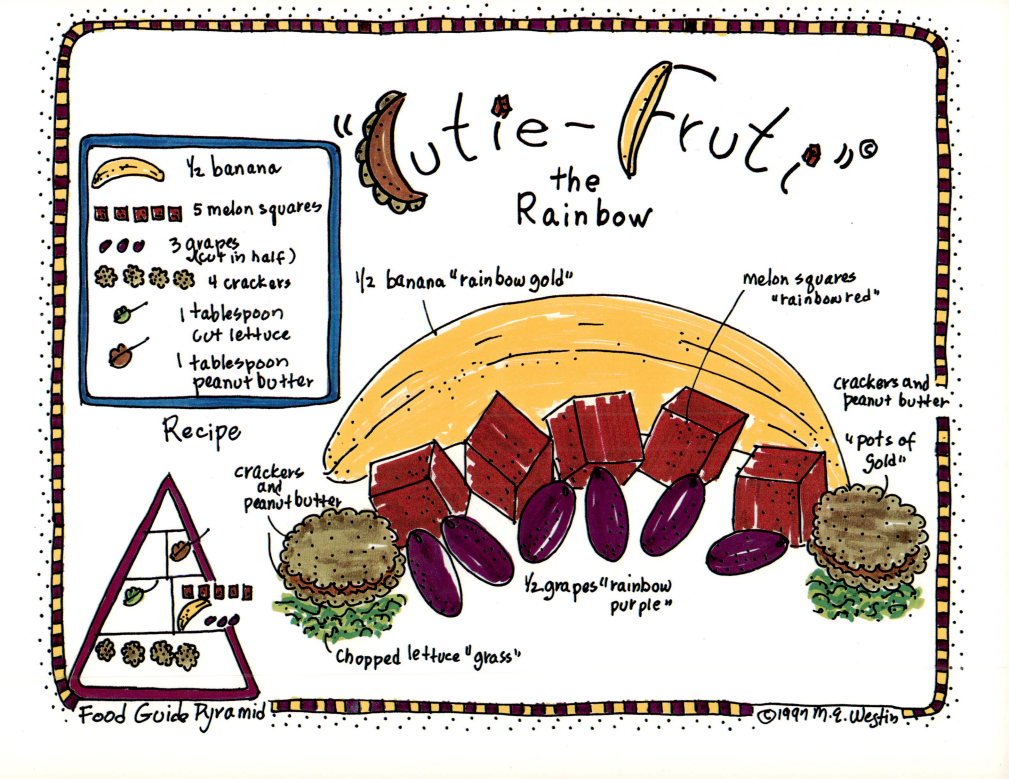

"Cutie-Fruti"© the Rainbow

Recipe

- ½ banana
- 5 melon squares
- 3 grapes (cut in half)
- 4 crackers
- 1 tablespoon cut lettuce
- 1 tablespoon peanut butter

½ banana "rainbow gold"

melon squares "rainbow red"

crackers and peanut butter

"pots of Gold"

crackers and peanut butter

½ grapes "rainbow purple"

Chopped lettuce "grass"

Food Guide Pyramid

"Icy" the Snowman
Snack-tivities

Food Patterns

5 peas

6 small raisins

3 Carrot rectangles — 1" long, 1/4"

2 tablespoon yogurt

1 bread circle 1 1/2"

1 bread circle 2 1/2"

1 carrot square — 1/2" x 1/2", 1/4"

1 melon square — 1" x 1", 1/4"

1 celery stick — 3" long, 1/2" thick

Food For Thought

1. How many different foods can you find? Can you name them?

2. How many different shapes can you find? Can you name them?

3. How many different colors can you find? Can you name them?

4. What other foods could you use in this recipe?

Step-by-Step

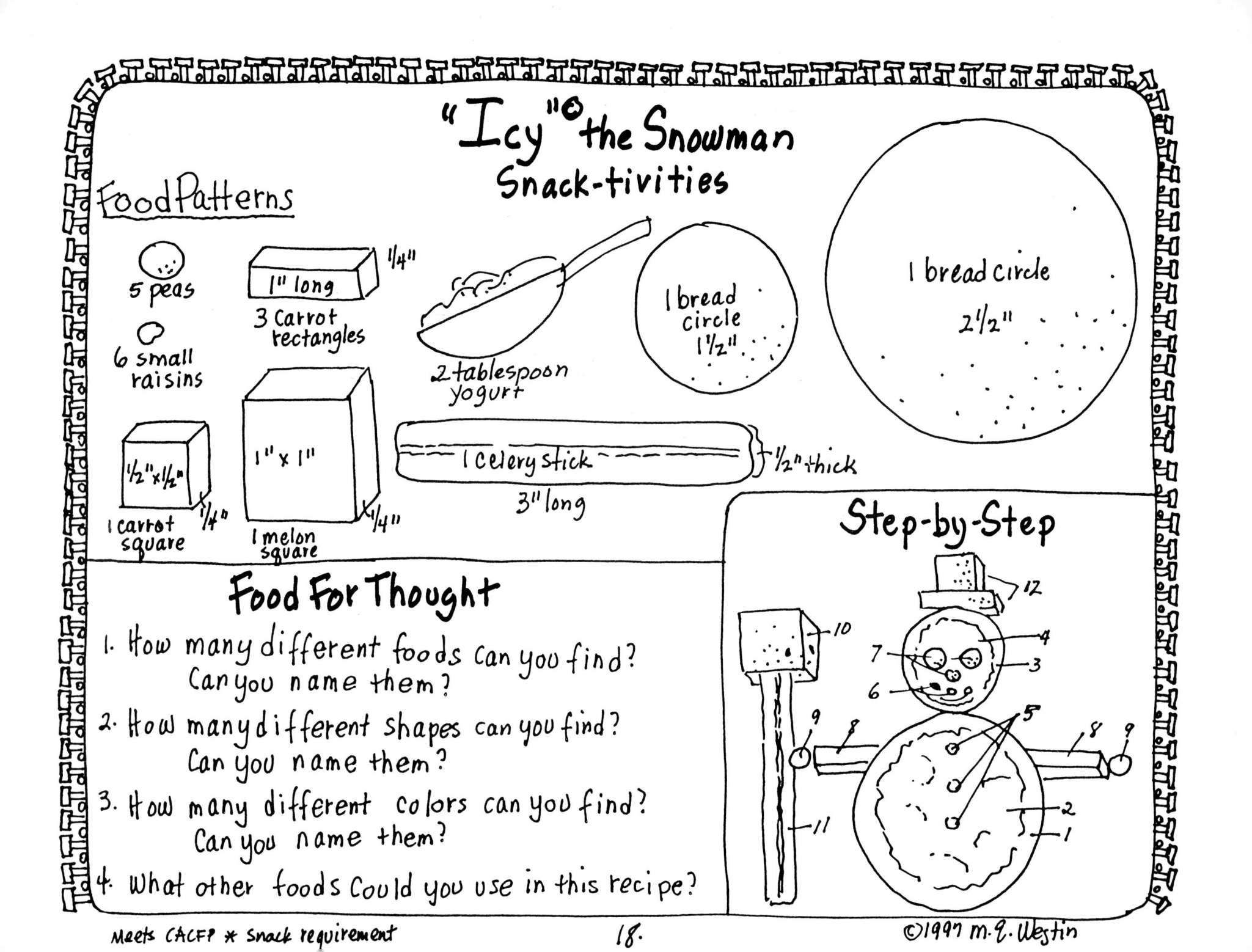

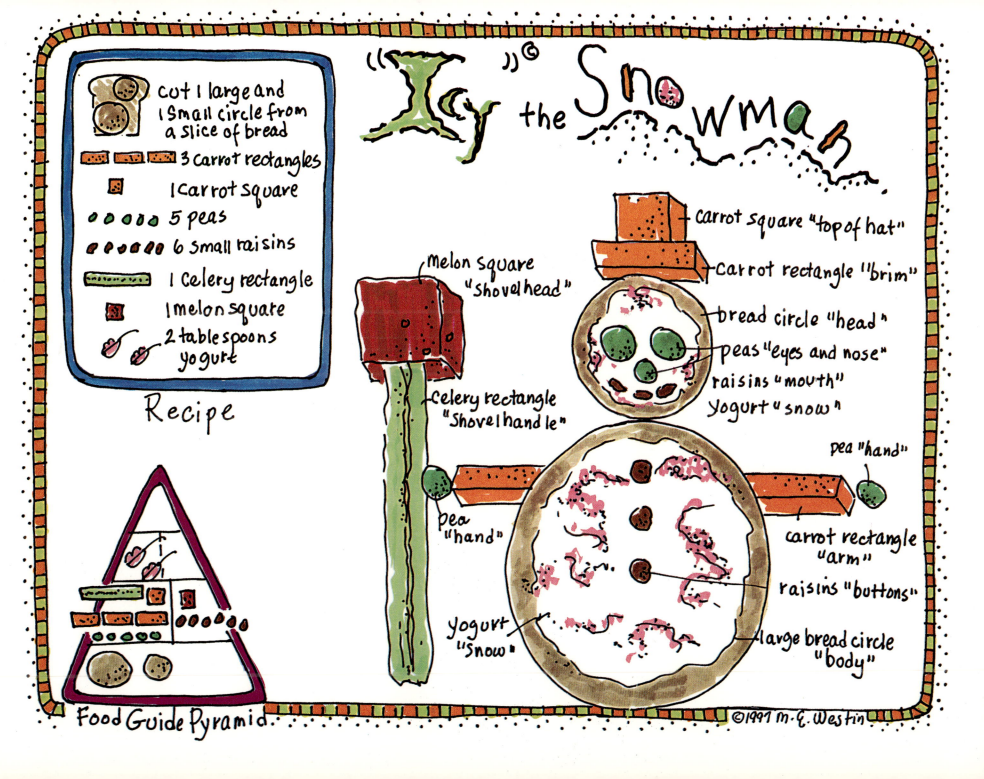

"Icy" the Snowman

Recipe

- cut 1 large and 1 small circle from a slice of bread
- 3 carrot rectangles
- 1 carrot square
- 5 peas
- 6 small raisins
- 1 celery rectangle
- 1 melon square
- 2 tablespoons yogurt

Food Guide Pyramid

melon square "shovel head"

celery rectangle "shovel handle"

pea "hand"

carrot square "top of hat"

carrot rectangle "brim"

bread circle "head"

peas "eyes and nose"

raisins "mouth"

yogurt "snow"

pea "hand"

carrot rectangle "arm"

raisins "buttons"

large bread circle "body"

yogurt "snow"

© 1997 M. E. Westin

"Lettuce Tail"© the Pony
Snack-tivities

Food Patterns

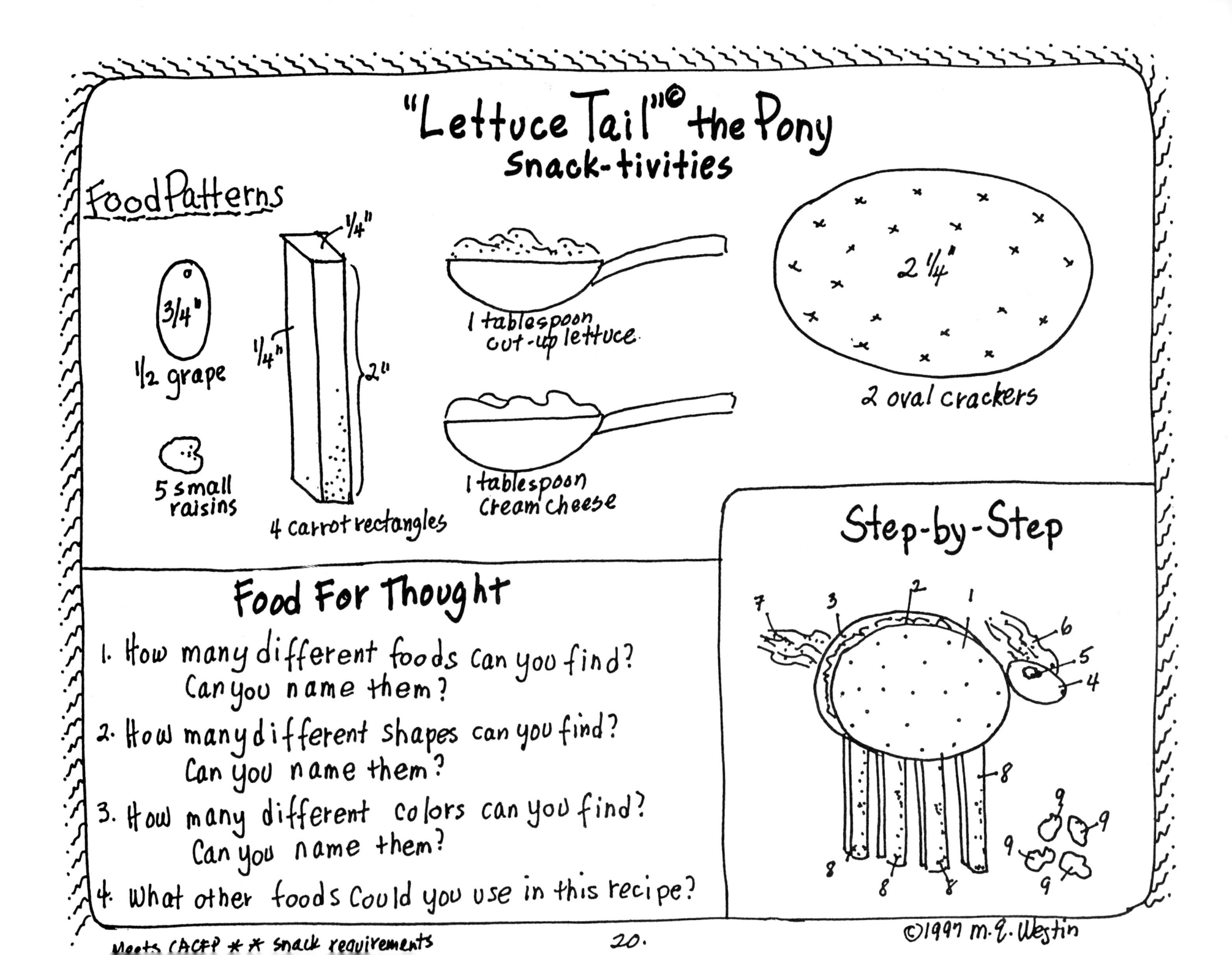

3/4"
½ grape

5 small raisins

¼"
¼"
2"
4 carrot rectangles

1 tablespoon cut-up lettuce

1 tablespoon cream cheese

2 ¼"
2 oval crackers

Food For Thought

1. How many different foods can you find? Can you name them?

2. How many different shapes can you find? Can you name them?

3. How many different colors can you find? Can you name them?

4. What other foods could you use in this recipe?

Step-by-Step

"Lettuce 'Tail'" the Pony

cream cheese "glue food"

lettuce "tail"

lettuce "mane"

raisin "eye"

½ grape "head"

crackers "body"

Carrot rectangles "legs"

raisins "pony food"

Recipe

2 oval crackers	
4 carrot rectangles	
½ grape	
5 small raisins	
1 tablespoon cut lettuce	
1 tablespoon cream cheese	

Food Guide Pyramid

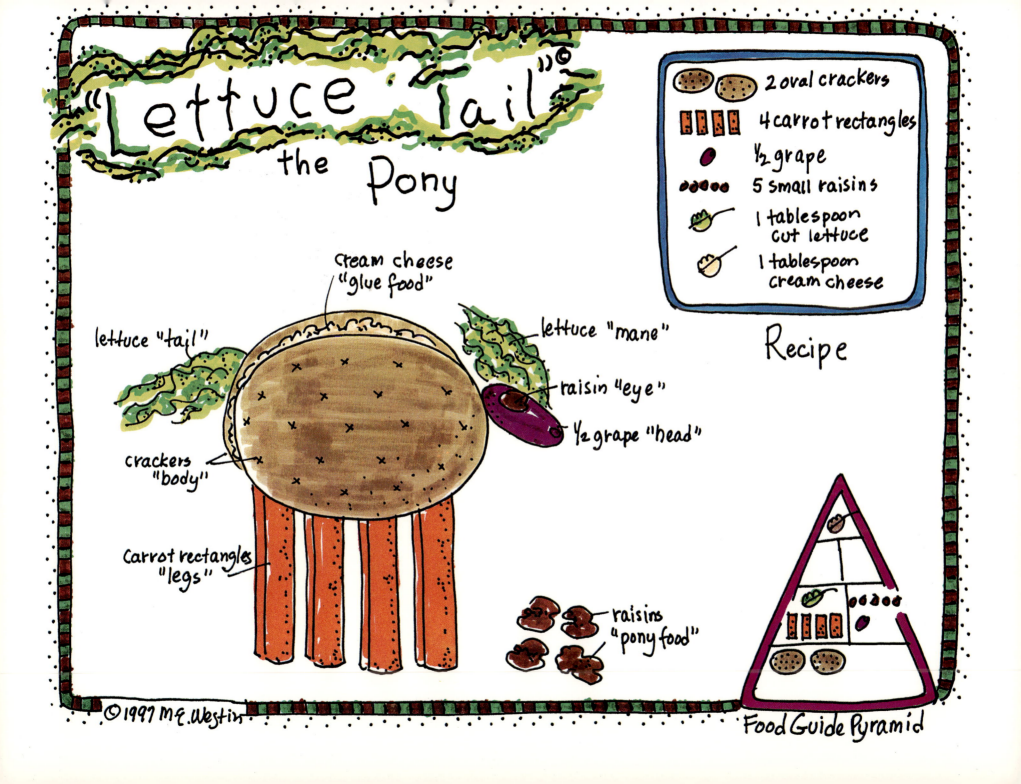

"Little Bite"© the Teddy Bear
Snack-tivities

Food Patterns

3 peas

½ carrot circle

¼" thick
4 carrot circles

1 grape
(cut into 2 halves)

1 - ¾" strawberry

2 tablespoons
cream cheese

1 - 1½" bread circle

1 - 2½" bread circle

Food For Thought

1. How many different foods can you find?
   Can you name them?

2. How many different shapes can you find?
   Can you name them?

3. How many different colors can you find?
   Can you name them?

4. What other foods could you use in this recipe?

Step-by-Step

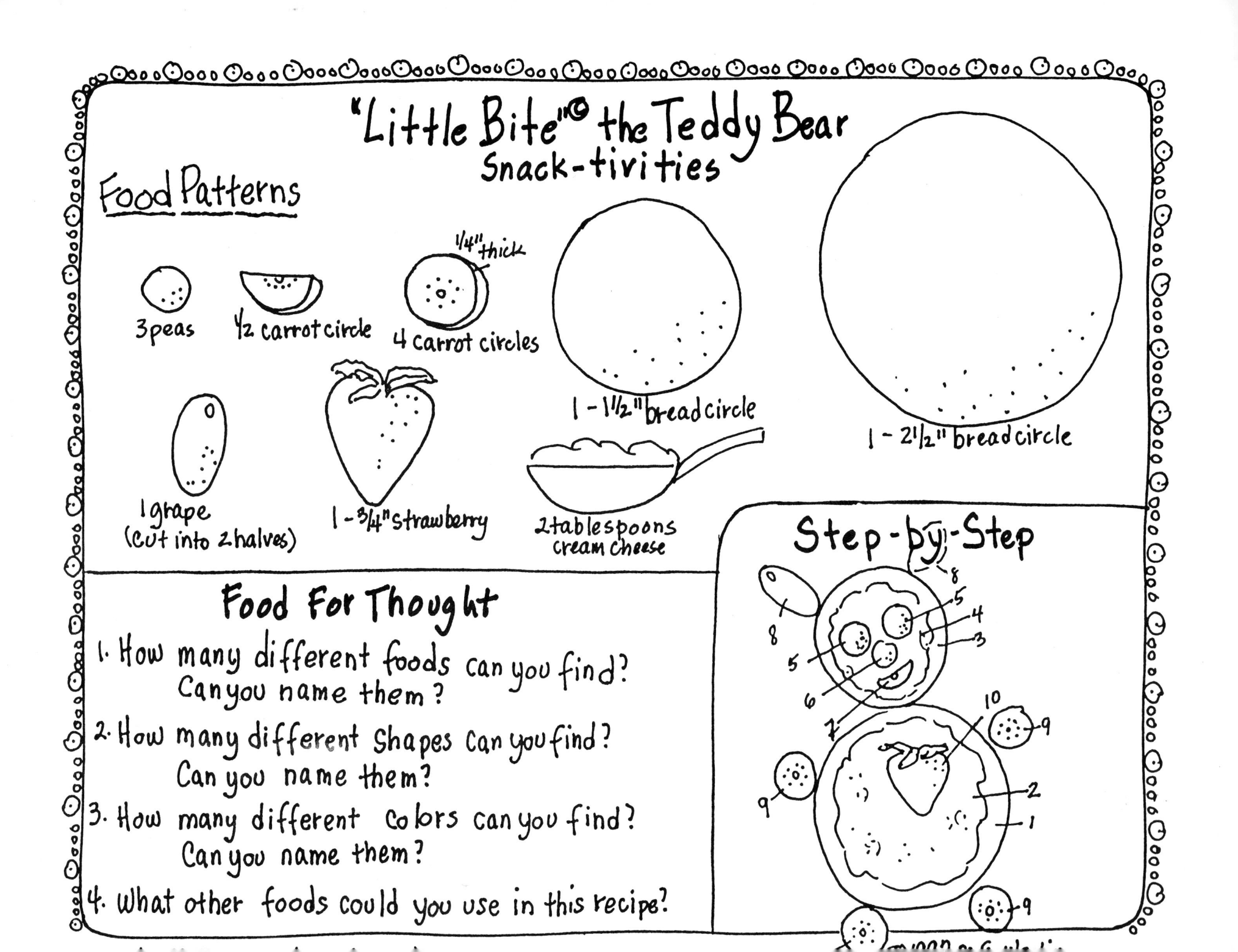

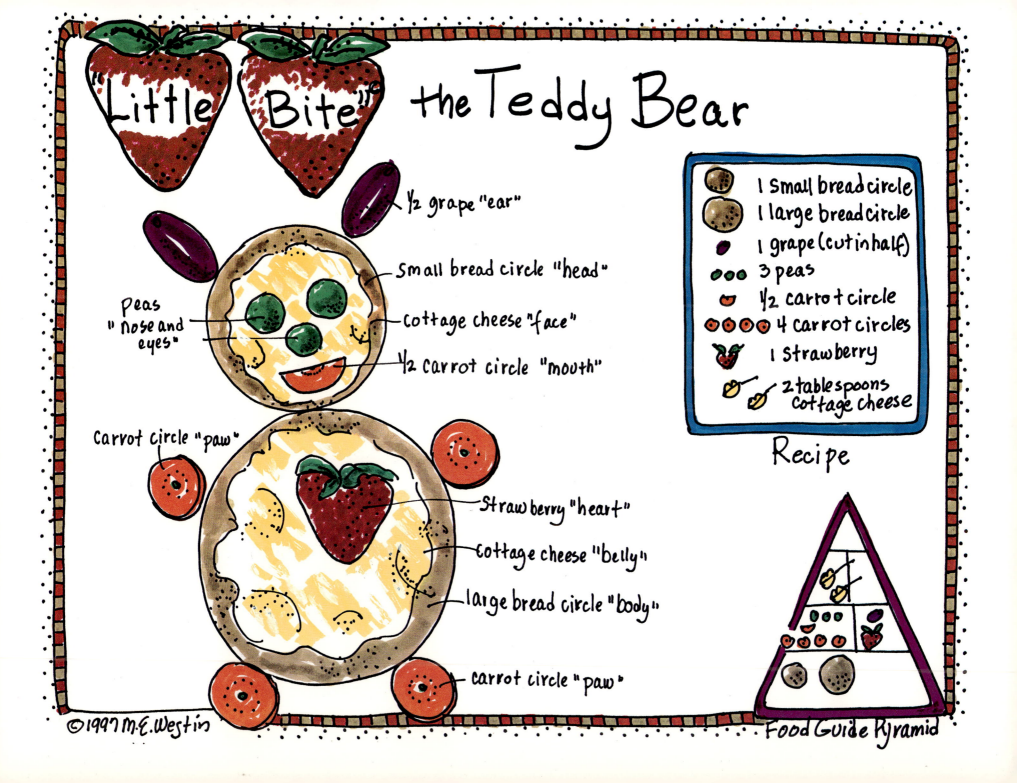

"Little Bite" the Teddy Bear

½ grape "ear"

Small bread circle "head"

Peas "nose and eyes"

cottage cheese "face"

½ carrot circle "mouth"

Carrot circle "paw"

Strawberry "heart"

cottage cheese "belly"

large bread circle "body"

carrot circle "paw"

Recipe

- 1 small bread circle
- 1 large bread circle
- 1 grape (cut in half)
- 3 peas
- ½ carrot circle
- 4 carrot circles
- 1 Strawberry
- 2 tablespoons cottage cheese

Food Guide Pyramid

©1997 M.E. Westin

"Pepper-horn" the Bull
Snack-tivities

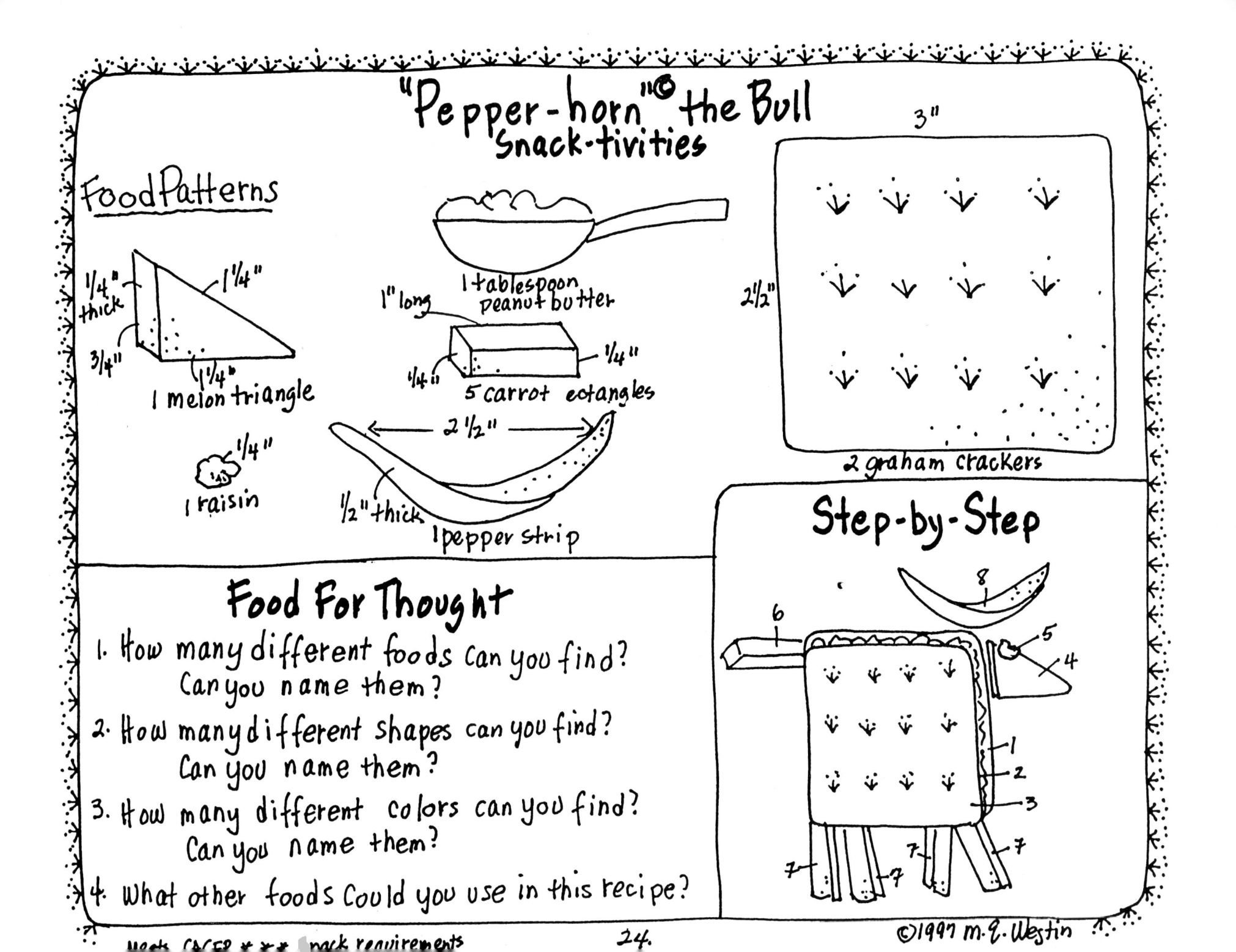

Food Patterns

1/4" thick
1 1/4"
3/4"
1 1/4"
1 melon triangle

1/4"
1 raisin

1 tablespoon peanut butter

1" long
1/4"
1/4"
5 carrot ectangles

2 1/2"
1/2" thick
1 pepper strip

3"
2 1/2"
2 graham crackers

Step-by-Step

6
8
5
4
1
2
3
7
7
7

Food For Thought

1. How many different foods can you find?
   Can you name them?

2. How many different shapes can you find?
   Can you name them?

3. How many different colors can you find?
   Can you name them?

4. What other foods could you use in this recipe?

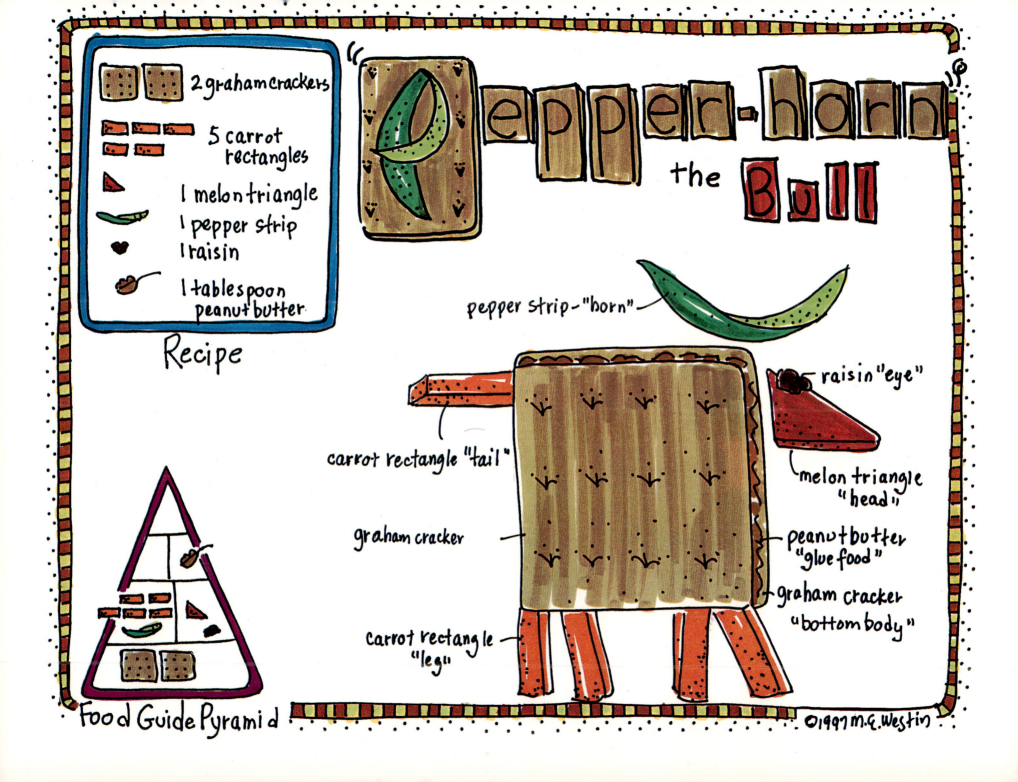

"Pepper-horn" the Bull

Recipe

- 2 graham crackers
- 5 carrot rectangles
- 1 melon triangle
- 1 pepper strip
- 1 raisin
- 1 tablespoon peanut butter

Food Guide Pyramid

pepper strip–"horn"

raisin "eye"

carrot rectangle "tail"

melon triangle "head"

graham cracker

peanut butter "glue food"

graham cracker "bottom body"

carrot rectangle "leg"

©1997 M.G. Westin

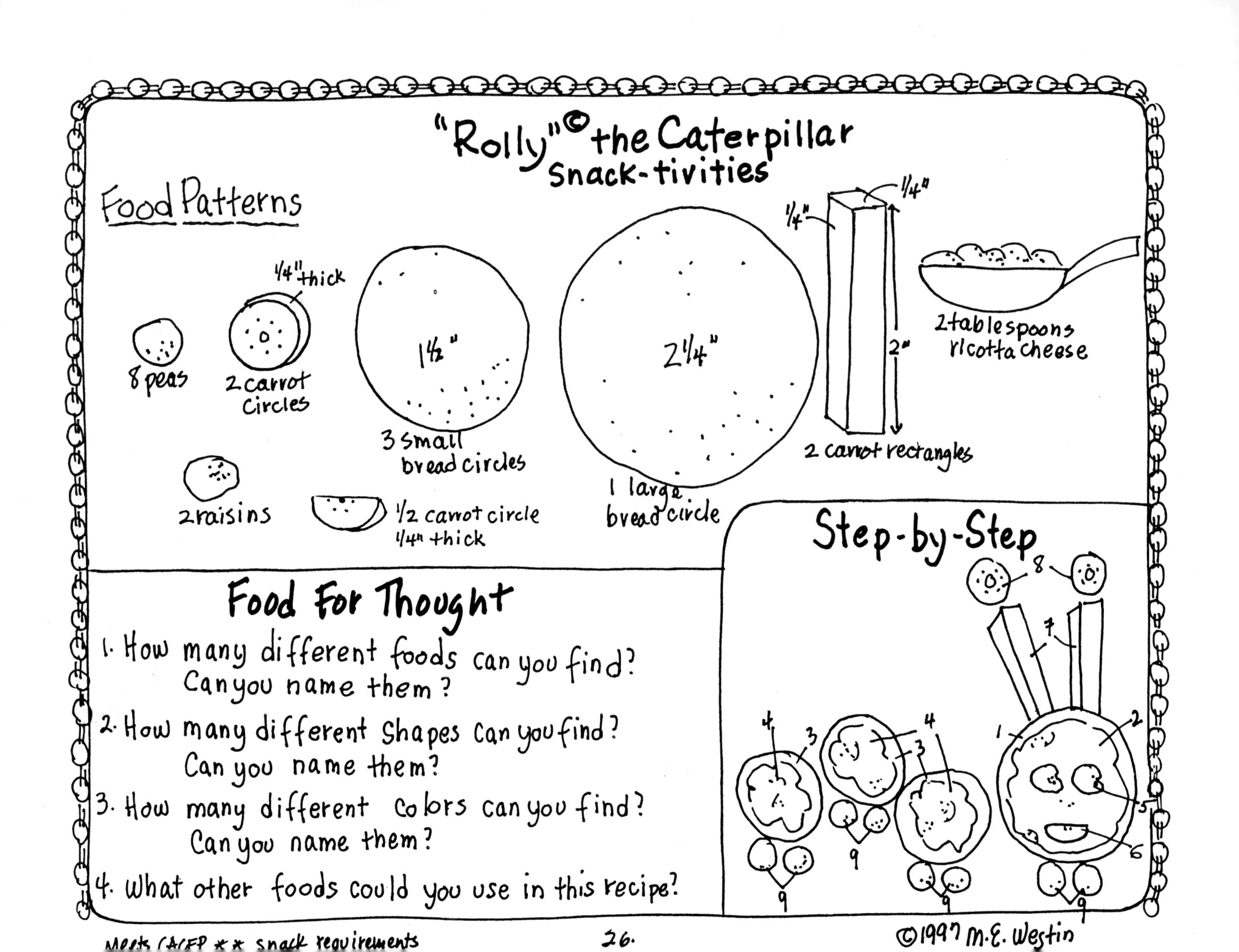

"Rolly" © the Caterpillar Snack-tivities

Food Patterns

8 peas

2 carrot circles — ¼" thick

3 small bread circles — 1½"

1 large bread circle — 2¼"

2 carrot rectangles — ¼" ¼" 2"

2 tablespoons ricotta cheese

2 raisins

½ carrot circle ¼" thick

Step-by-Step

Food For Thought

1. How many different foods can you find? Can you name them?

2. How many different shapes can you find? Can you name them?

3. How many different colors can you find? Can you name them?

4. What other foods could you use in this recipe?

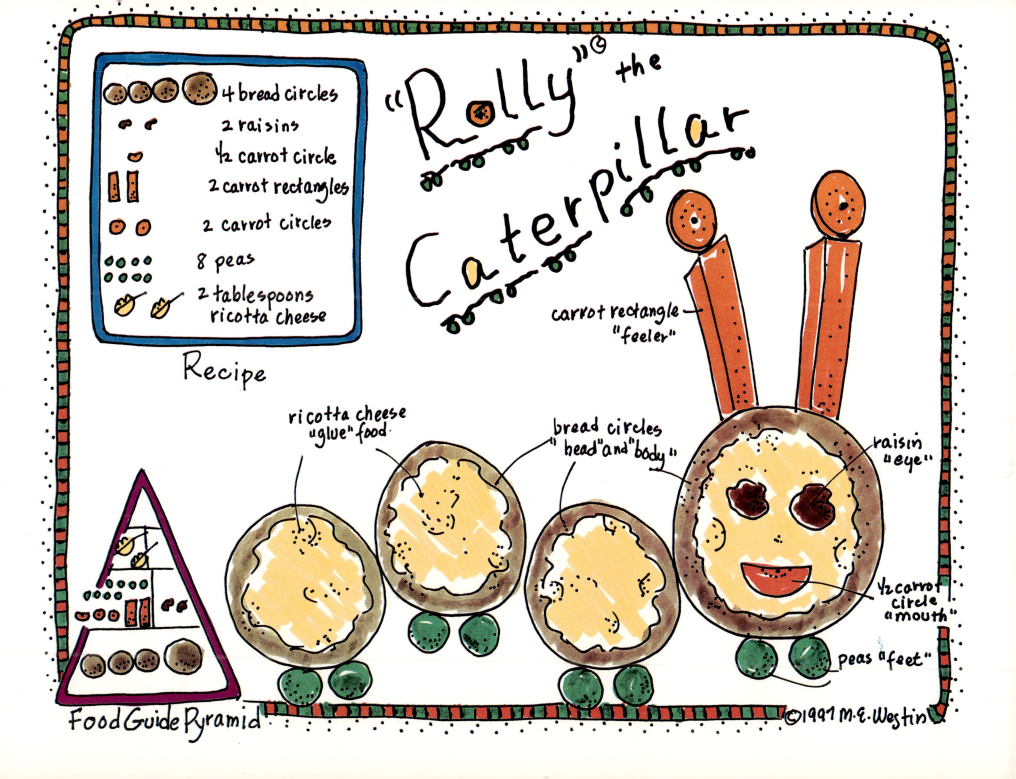

"Rolly" the Caterpillar

Recipe

- 4 bread circles
- 2 raisins
- ½ carrot circle
- 2 carrot rectangles
- 2 carrot circles
- 8 peas
- 2 tablespoons ricotta cheese

carrot rectangle "feeler"

ricotta cheese "glue" food

bread circles "head" and "body"

raisin "eye"

½ carrot circle "mouth"

peas "feet"

Food Guide Pyramid

©1997 M.E. Westin

"Wisher" the Star
Snack-tivities

Food Patterns

3/4" size

3 grapes
(Cut in half to make 6 pieces)

1/8" circle

1/4" thick

6 banana circles

2 1/2"

5 tortilla triangles

1/4" thick

2 1/4"

1 orange slice

Step-by-Step

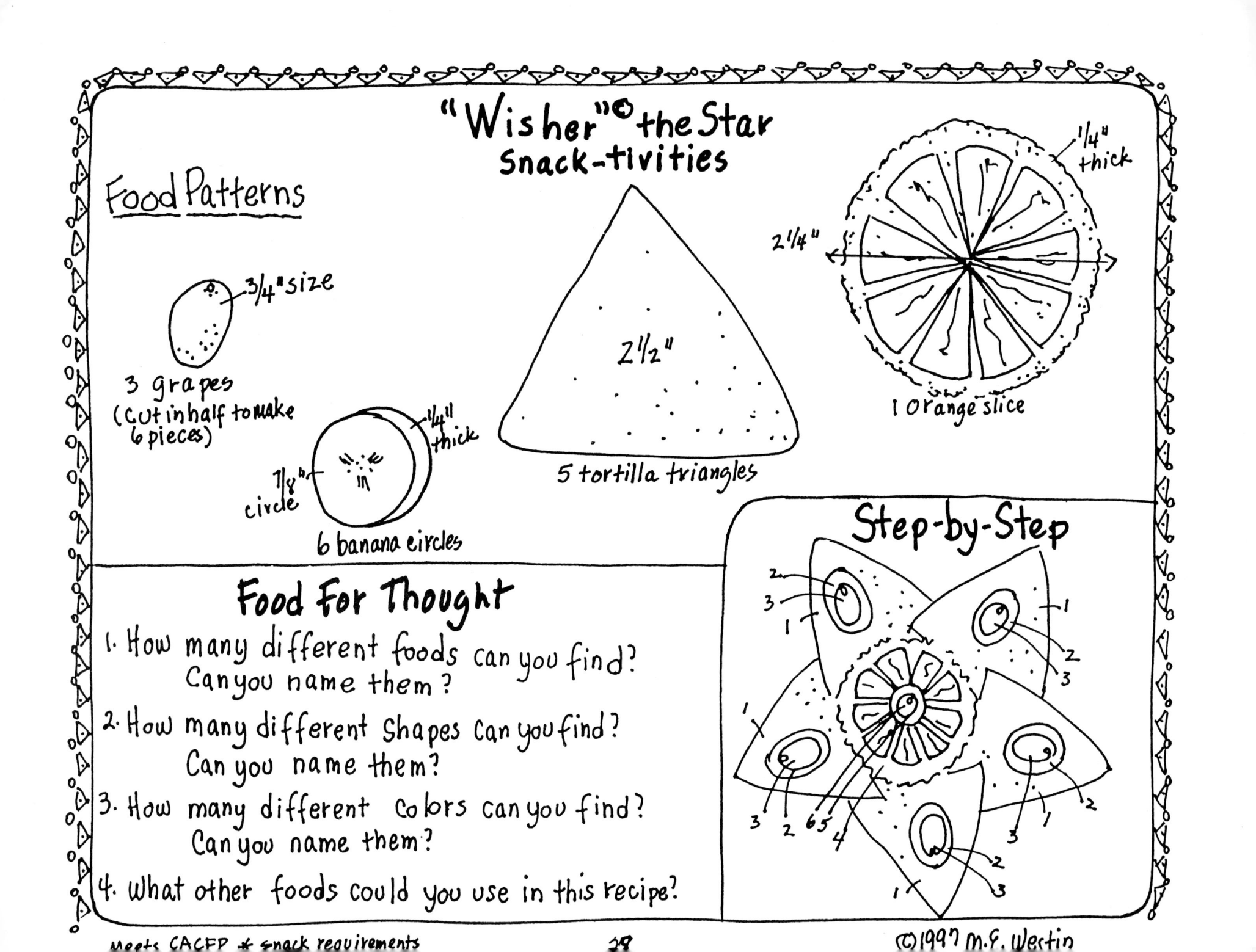

Food For Thought

1. How many different foods can you find? Can you name them?

2. How many different shapes can you find? Can you name them?

3. How many different colors can you find? Can you name them?

4. What other foods could you use in this recipe?

"Wisher"© the Star

banana circles "star glow"

orange slice "star center"

tortilla triangles "star points"

½ grape "star glow"

5 tortilla triangles

1 orange slice

6 banana circles

3 grapes (cut into 6 halves)

Recipe

©1997 M.E. Wghln

Food Guide Pyramid

CUTTING AND PREPARATION IDEAS

Apples, bananas, grapes 31
Recipe abbreviations 31
Bagels, bread slices, bread sticks, crackers, ... 32
    pretzels and tortilla triangles 32
Oranges, raisins, strawberries, watermellon 33
Fruit, servings per day 33
Carrots, celery, lettuce, green beans, peas 34
Vegetables, servings per day 34
Peppers, cheese 35
Common measurements and equivalents 35
                        and
More Snack Ideas .36

Apple

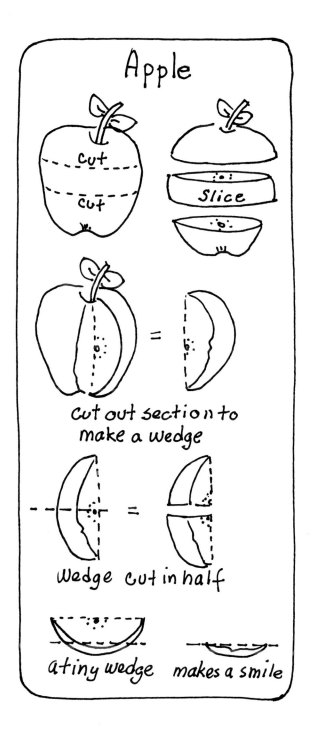

cut

cut

Slice

cut out section to
make a wedge

=

wedge cut in half

=

a tiny wedge   makes a smile

Banana

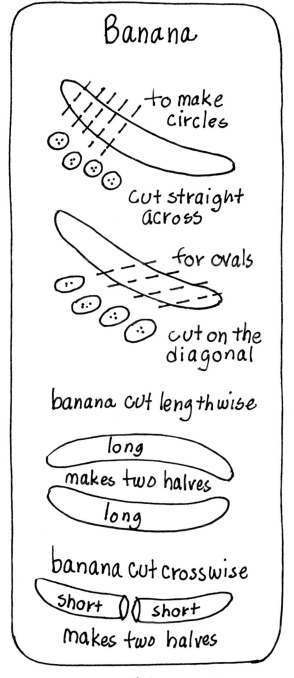

to make
circles

Cut straight
across

for ovals

cut on the
diagonal

banana cut lengthwise

long

makes two halves

long

banana cut crosswise

short   short

makes two halves

Grapes

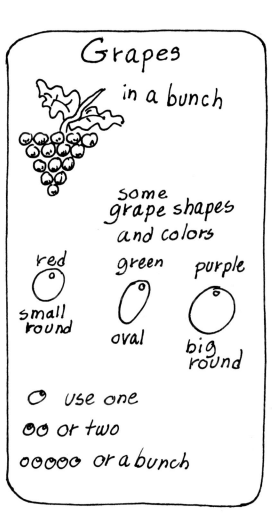

in a bunch

some
grape shapes
and colors

red

green

purple

small
round

oval

big
round

use one

or two

or a bunch

Question:
How long did it take
you to make your
Put-Together© snack?

Bagels

whole   or   cut in half

two halves

If you cut the halves crosswise, you will get...

4 pieces to eat!

Breads

There are many different types... and shapes

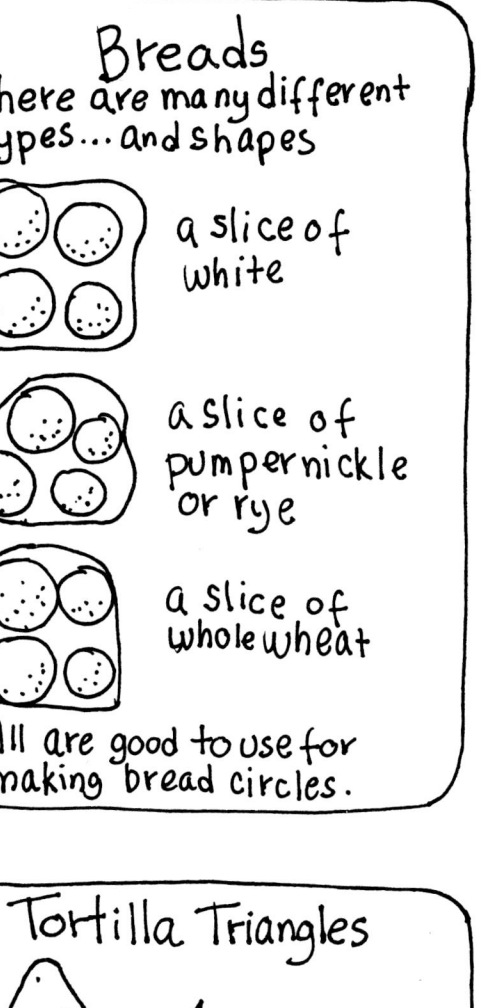

a slice of white

a slice of pumpernickle or rye

a slice of whole wheat

All are good to use for making bread circles.

Crackers

Can you recognize these basic shapes? How many ways can you use them?

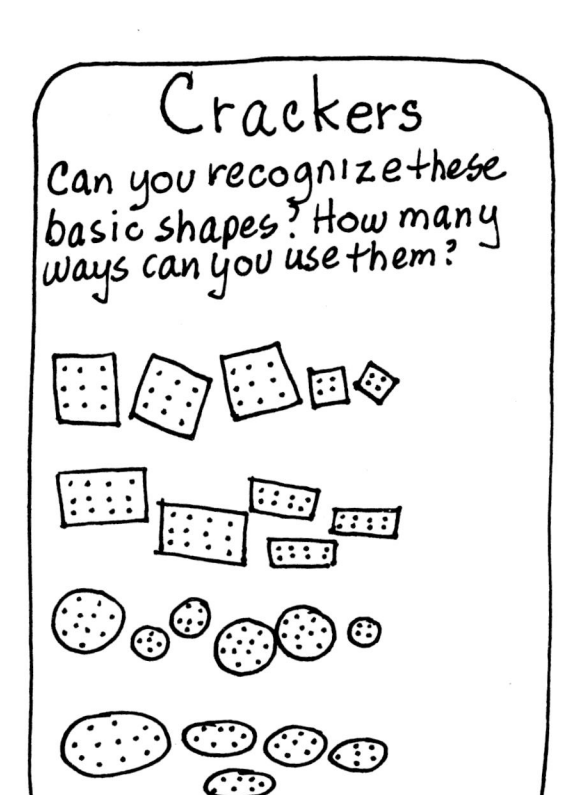

Bread Sticks

long and fat, or

long and thin

Tortilla Triangles

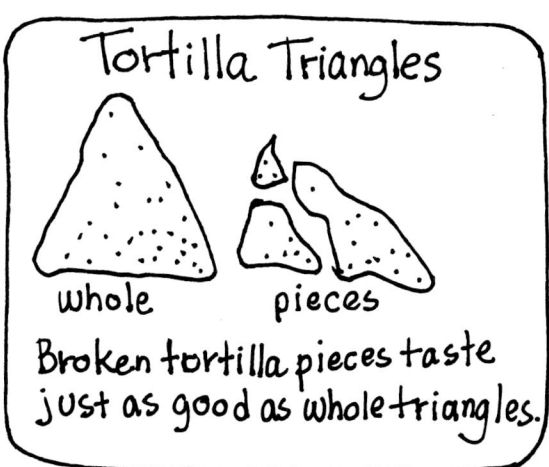

whole   pieces

Broken tortilla pieces taste just as good as whole triangles.

Pretzels

Crunchier than bread sticks
Lots of choices

twisted

long and thick
short and thin
nuggets

Orange

The whole orange

A cut orange top

middle slice

bottom

An orange slice lying flat

The rind is on the outside. It is bitter, don't eat it.

A half slice

Raisins

These funny looking fruits are really dried grapes

big

small

They can be used in many different places in our recipes

Strawberry

Look at your strawberry. Does it have a triangle shape?

The Food Guide Pyramid suggests that you eat 2-4 servings of fruit each day.

Watermelon

seed

first cut a slice

separate the melon from

the rind (do not eat)

cut the shape you need

Some other melons that you may use are:

Cantaloupe
honeydew

Can you think of other melons?

33.

Carrots

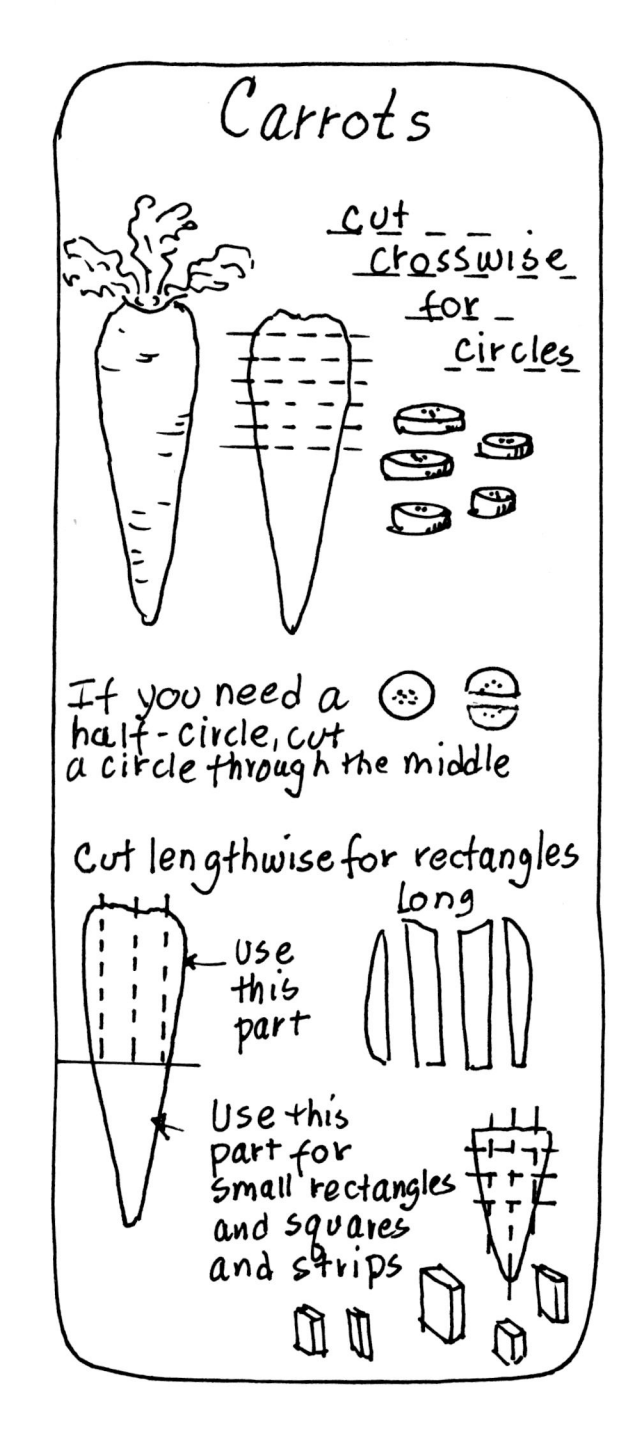

cut crosswise for circles

If you need a half-circle, cut a circle through the middle

Cut lengthwise for rectangles

long

← use this part

Use this part for small rectangles and squares and strips

Celery

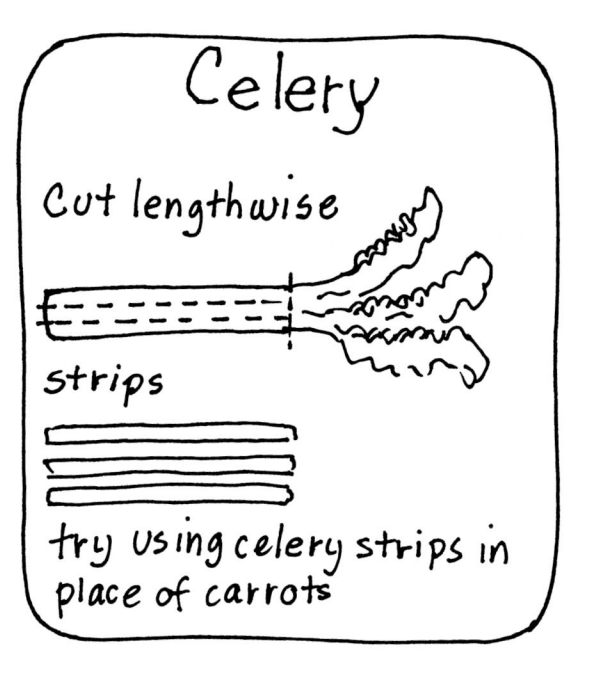

Cut lengthwise

strips

try using celery strips in place of carrots

Lettuce Leaf

Cut leaves crosswise to get long, wavy strips.

lettuce tastes good when cut very thin

Green Beans

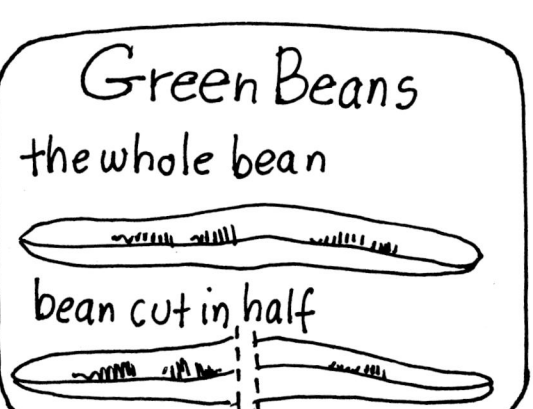

the whole bean

bean cut in half

The Food Guide Pyramid suggests that you eat 3-5 servings of vegetables each day.

Peas

They look like this in the pod

out of the pod

How many different ways can you think of to use peas in the recipes?

Peppers

They have many different colors, shapes and flavors.

This one is big and square, mild and sweet.

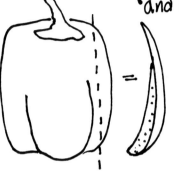

Cut pepper strip straight up and down.

This pepper is long and thin, spicy and hot!

The tiny, round ones are very very HOT!

Cheese

one square cut diagonally

makes two triangles

One square can make many different shapes

long rectangles
short rectangles
tiny squares

Common Measures and Equivalents

3 tsp. = 1 T

2 T = 1/8 cup

4 T = 1/4 cup

How many of these fruits and vegetables have you eaten?

pears   blueberries

cabbage

plantains   red beets

Kidney beans

radishes

soy beans

cucumbers

corn

spinach   okra

brussel sprouts

Which ones did we miss?

MORE SNACK IDEAS

ADD the missing food and create your own snack.

1. I can use carrots, grapes and ——— to make a good snack.

2. Green beans and ——— look like a ——— when I add cheese squares.

3. Melon triangles taste good when I eat them with ——— and ———.

4. If I choose grapes, tortilla triangles and ——— they make a ———.

5. Cottage cheese and raisins taste good with ———.

6. Banana circles and orange slices taste better when I add ———.

7. Crunchy pepper strips and ——— sound like ——— when I chew them.

Many thanks to the following Westchester County librarians who, by allowing us to present our food designs at their children'is programs, helped us gain valuable insight in developing these recipes.

Pam Morrison, Somers Public Library, Somers, N.Y.
Vicki Ingrassia, Katonah Public Library, Katonah, N.Y.
Miriam Boden, Mt. Kisco Public Library, Mt. Kisco, N.Y.
Susan Chajes, Mount Pleasant Public Library, Pleasantville, N.Y.

ABOUT THE AUTHORS

MARGARET E. WESTIN is a Home Economist with a specialization in design. She holds a BFA from Pratt Institute and an MA from New York University, with teaching experience at the pre-school, middle and high schools as well as undergraduate and graduate levels. She has authored various educational publications including a four volume multi-media series titled INTERIOR DESIGN, published by Butterick Marketing Co. and Chrome Yellow Films. Her pen illustrated the recipes in this book.

NORMAN W. WESTIN is an architect practicing in Mt. Kisco, N.Y. His long experience in line, form and composition proved extremely valuable in the creation of the visual format for this work. Working together, the authors developed this book as an expression of a life long interest in helping to introduce children to foods that not only taste good but are healthy and nutritious.